This Teeming Mess of Glory

This Teeming Mess of Glory

Matthew Pullar

RESOURCE *Publications* · Eugene, Oregon

THIS TEEMING MESS OF GLORY

Resource Publications
An Imprint of Wipf and Stock Publishers
199 W. 8th Ave., Suite 3
Eugene, OR 97401

www.wipfandstock.com

PAPERBACK ISBN: 979-8-3852-4225-2
HARDCOVER ISBN: 979-8-3852-4226-9
EBOOK ISBN: 979-8-3852-4227-6

VERSION NUMBER 012225

For my children

And God said, "Let the water teem with living creatures, and let birds fly above the earth across the vault of the sky."

~ Genesis 1:20 New International Version

The air was thick with teeming life, just as the oceans and the rivers were. A spoonful of seawater or a pinch of soil between your fingers held billions of living things. We were blind to this out of necessity, because if we saw what was really there we would never move. It was around us, between us, on the edge of us and inside us.

~ Martin MacInnes, In Ascension

Contents

Acknowledgments

Many thanks to:

Hannah, my constant companion through so much of this journey, and Elias, Dominic and Patrick, our shared treasures.

Andrew Lansdown, for the inspiration and insight.

D.S. Martin, for the encouragement and attentiveness to detail.

Laurie Klein, for the friendship and guidance, and for cheering me on across the globe.

Whitney Rio-Ross, for the generosity of support.

Sharmini Kumar, for continually hassling me to submit more of my poetry for publication, and for always championing my work.

These poems were written on the lands of the Yagumbeh, Wurundjeri, Bunurong and Boandik people, for the glory of God, the creator and sustainer of all things.

Thanks to the following journals and anthologies that previously published a number of these poems:

Proost Poets 2: Reaching for Mercy: "Homecoming"

Home + Content: "Northbound on Derrimut"

Soul Tread: "A Work of Love"

Poems for Ephesians: "Dianoia" and "Bathos":

Reformed Journal: "Vespers: After Louise Gluck" and "Life Beneath"

Ekstasis: "Breathbodyprayer"

"Someday All This Will Be Yours" received an honorable mention in the 2024 Fare Forward Poetry Competition and was published in *Fare Forward*.

Many of these poems formed part of my unpublished manuscript "Imperceptible Arms", for which I received the SparkLit Young Australian Christian Writer of the Year in 2012.

All Bible quotations, unless otherwise noted, are from the King James Version. The epigraph is from the New International Version.

Readers should note that these poems include discussions of mental illness as well as colonisation. I pray they might be a source of healing for any who struggle with the weight of these things.

I
Soil

Sight, smell and sound are discovered here.
First memory's a summit in sepia thought;
I take my first steps in this basalted earth,
red like blood, like lava, in the mountain's veins.
Settlers misheard the name for this place:
Jambreen—a finger-lime, mistaken for
a tambourine, shaking jubilant,
sounding its praise in the dawn of my days.
Everything starts here, knee-deep in grass,
rising golden in sun, as though birthed on this hill.
Settlers saw the warning and did not heed;
and so I am here, in a town misnamed,
in a life and a body I have yet to learn,
fresh to assume the volcanic world.

Bounding

Into the treetops I fly in my singing, all
green and fresh bounding, the heights of my laughter.

The sun in its climbing brings life to the rafters; I
dance over rooftops of houses and canopies.

Listen: my birthday is come; I am newly born.
Death has been flung to its deep forest grave.

Home

It snowed the week I was born; my brother
and sister, fresh from Sydney, harvested
July joy with tingling fingers, gathered
what they could in eager clumps and pressed it
like ice cream into a punnet, to freeze
and store for future play. I missed the fun,
born a week late, but days of ten degrees
trained me for cold; when we moved to the northern sun,
home was too hazy in the summer steam.
I chased winter instead of heat. The first sigh
of frozen breath, I puffed my Arctic wish,
ignoring gumtrees that caught me in my lie.
Home is what our aspirations miss,
where daydreams stop and cognisance is bliss.

Grace, eight or nine years old

A lonely night;
guilt like fetters
(unexpected; unexplained)
enclosing.
A burst of tears:
my spirit's rain;
the knowledge—hard
and sudden—that
this is me:
a sight of me
unknown to me,
fetid, enfettered,
enflamed.

Yet from space
and nothing, grace
as lovehand reaches,
takes, embraces
deeper than skin,
deeper than
muscles, and
massages heartstrings.
Joyful, I sing.
(Is this all
no more than a
child's half-sleeping
fancy? I cannot tell,
but this I know:
my heart then leapt
and rejoiced like
never before.)

The Mountain

I.

The school beneath the mountain where I play
stands at the still point of the leaping road.
Our stomachs fall and ears seal up as we
make daily treks down tracks where goats were led.
The lizard boy is there when I arrive;
he smells always of poo from that one day;
and Sam as well who clenched his fist when toys
caused war upon our meeting, then instead
formed alliance with me on the slide.
"I miss Sam," I'll cry when, in Grade Three,
I join my siblings' school down on the coast
and both of us have lost these mountain joys,
Sam gone with his mum to join another man
and me in deference to my parents' plans.

II.
So swift the road, so brutal on the brakes.
at first I play, delighted in the day,
and then I spy my mother walk away.
The first betrayal: a giving lost in take.
Was this what we'd agreed? Were these high stakes
all part of why she lured me to play
with slippery slide and monkey bars? No way.
I brawl my protest in deep howls and shakes.
How do we two negotiate from here?
Memory's vague on details. Perhaps this
letting go is our primary lesson.
Hold on and let go. The incline is sheer.
My mother controls the brakes as we press on,
Uniting, departing. . .
        What's growing? This is.

Topography

. . .rediscovering, room by room, what it was that I first learned
there about how high, how wide the world is, how one space opens
into another. . .

~ *David Malouf*, 12 Edmondstone Street

How many of my dreams go to this place?
Always the same Queenslander balconies
where I wander over those drooping eaves
in search of silent, drowsy days of grace.
What do I find there? Memory's faint trace,
nestled somewhere in the comfort of leaves,
world always higher than my eyes believe.
I must always look up to see Your face,
so dreams look up too: to canopy, to farm
atop a hill, a volcanic red dome. . .
When I return here with my wife, we find
the colors that I know, the trilling sound
of butcherbird above our heads, yet my mind
always says, "Climb up. This is still not the ground."

The Grandparents Quartet

Stuart Simmers Pullar (1910-1999)

Teenager, having no experience of death or its proximity, I
am ill-equipped for what lies before me:
my grandfather, wizened by Alzheimer's, and my
ever-private grandmother stroking
his hand while she recounts the days
lived together. And what days.
Decades, beginning in Melbourne, then Fiji,
Queensland, Newcastle, quiver filling as they went.
It's years until I learn that once,
my father still a child, Grandad nearly
took a job in the centre, at Tennant Creek. My own
decades have flown by then and I, nearing forty,
my own quiver full, wander
the Tennant Creek caravan park, past
a display of the old mining days and try
to conceive of my father—the man I know, not
as happenstance might have made him—
living and growing here. I catch
the fancy as it flies. Had he moved here, he
would not be my father. How the future teeters
on precarious things. My mere act of
being depends on his family's final
journey south to Sydney where
my parents meet, marry, make my sister,
my brother, and me. Many
miscarriages in between. Life miscarries. Lives
carry on. "We've had a wonderful life," Gran says.
"No-one needs to be sad when I die."
Grandad, looking at his wife's hand stroking his,
croaks a rare interjection: "You'll wear

8

a hole in it." Gran, though satisfied
with years well spent, cannot
quite let go. Wears a hole.
Wears it whole.

Elisabeth Lucy Pullar (1915-2005)

She wore a tweed skirt wherever she went, walking
to enjoy the solitude and quietly
grumpy if a well-meaning neighbour offered a lift.
An Anglican from birth, she despised
the greeting of peace, deeming it
an excuse for mid-service socializing

At her 90th I caught on my camera
a moment of her face staring in wonder at the family
around her. "All these tall men," she marvelled. And I remember
the pride I felt the day I measured
five foot in my PE class and couldn't wait
for Christmas to stand taller than Gran.
                              More fool me.
On Christmas Day, she announced, with a chuckle,
that osteoporosis had made her shrink.
I had outgrown her before I even knew.

Yet never outgrew
the strength she hid in her dainty
elderly-lady-of-the-Highlands look.
A new mother in Fiji during
a world war, her own mother on
the other side of Bass Strait cried,
"Oh, poor Betty", with the news
of each subsequent child. She carried
seven to birth, six to adulthood, her middle son
never waking from anaesthetic when
my father—her youngest—was days old.
Carried on. Never said
aloud when she disagreed: sometimes
whistled. Never used the word grace yet burnt
a pile of hurt-filled letters when God
told her to. Opened her heart.
So many tall men. She dwarfed us all.

James Adam John Savage (1921-2007)

Hellraiser when young, he was known
as Tombstone to his airforce friends,
told the tale when I was a child of the wild
wartime night when he stole a tombstone
from a churchyard and earned his name.
Proud of his spirit, confused by the signs
of a wildness I did not understand, could not
condone, I preferred the tamer
elderly gentleman I knew, purveyor of fine
teas and foods, teaching my pallet to savour
Lapsang Souchong and blue vein cheese,
lilting Dickens and Burns to my eager ears, and,
as I grew, showing me the ways
of a camera's shutter with light.
As I took in the first rays of adulthood, we spoke
of Polanski, Steinbeck, Marquez.
"I'll miss our chats," he said from his final
hospital bed. Almost two decades now and still
eyes moisten. He opened them.
Still, still, I take in the light.

Kathleen Mary Savage (1929-2020)

Weeks before the world closed, I flew
back and forth from my city to hers, never
sure which time would be my last. Sometimes
she cried at the sight of me, cried
when I left. Sometimes she slept.
Once I watched her sleep, while beyond
the thin blue curtain another
grandmother grieved and moaned
while her grandson failed to grasp her grief.
Family wounds festered, untended, on their side, while my
grandmother sunk into snores.

Widowed thirteen years, time never
sat easily with her since losing him.
Days seemed vacant. Love for him
bonded us. In her last days we sometimes
simply spoke of him. But only in
his absence did I start to see her fully, and now
despite my parents' constant cautions—
She won't be herself; you won't
know how you'll find her—I kept
returning for the mere sight of her,
as long as she lingered.

The last time we spoke, she
pronounced her utter despair. Said it
again, again, like a judgement. I know
I said goodbye. I think we understood.
Next and last time she didn't wake. I kissed
her forehead. I heard death rasp
but didn't catch it. We knew
by then of aerosols. I would only fly
one more time that year, or the next.
Jesus loves you, I choked. So do I.
Perhaps she heard. Never stirred.

The See-Saw

The motion pulls us this way and that, astride
a swaying plank of ever moving force,
and how we go, how you and I both ride
the gambit and the sure and certain course
is now to trust and now to hold our arms
beside our sides as slowly we both bend,
never safe yet always far from harm,
the only certainty that this will end.
Now up, now down, the movement takes us all
in dips and troughs and soaring heights, to trees;
there's special providence in sparrow's fall
and quantum joy within the rushing breeze;
and by the see-saw's side my father stands,
gently reaching with his shaking hands.

Arms I

Sometimes I am small,
a package of tightly bundled
wayward retracting
into the clenched beating
of praying fists.

This is not humble, though
it feints and mumbles like it was,
with sounds of prayers like
knuckles uncurling, knees buckled,
muscles tense from much closing.

When I am small again,
I bid that You might take my arms
and stretch them out till bones are straight.
Then, then, I will learn to raise them
to your warm and holy sky.

Vespers: After Louise Glück

Once I believed in You,
still do,
though belief is often evasive, often abstract,
like air, which itself defies grasp
yet needy lungs clutch at it with the certainty
that this, this alone they must have.

And I believe like
the fig tree believes in the soil,
sometimes wilted, sometimes refusing fruit,
always held, always known to the roots.

And at the vesper light, I
believe, not with
the confident certainty of the apologist in debate,
the smug politician turning
divine name to unholy cause,
but like
the bed beneath me believes in the ground,
believes in the frame that holds it.

For all your unwritten poems

This one has a stone wall that you saw
driving north at sunrise on your last day at work.
You thought, "I'll write a poem about that", but by sunset
it was lockdown again
and you went home to stay home. No poem.

This one has a glimpse
you caught of your face reflected in a sunlit window
and your freckles surprised even you, as though
the last time you'd seen yourself you were pale
and now time and slowness had put their pigment on you.
You began—a sonnet, if I recall correct—but never finished,
the iambs too regular, life
in too much quiet disarray for that.

This one has ivy winding around it,
and this one got lost taking out the compost.
These ones were bundled together in your bed
when you fell asleep, and this one lies tangled
in your youngest son's cot.
Over there's an epic that was never thought
and under the garden path is a song.
"Remember us?" these cry, as you hang laundry to dry
and somewhere, yes somewhere, you're sure that you do.

When it works,
when the sounds and pictures and words combine
to take shape on a page, on a screen, on a tongue,
you will look up, and find the stone wall has become a city,
the compost heap an orchard, vast,
your children resting beneath the boughs.

You will stand
on the bedrock of your unwritten thoughts,
teeming with miles of living humus beneath you,
everything being written, all the while.

II
Water

Above the surface only shimmers,
faint disturbance in the water's field, only
the ripples of the moon's pull and release.
Nothing belies what lies beneath,
and world with its snorkel has scarcely seen
the vast trenches teeming with archaea,
protozoic ooze replete with a hundred
trillion untold poems on the verge of living.
Life, the scientist says, will find a way.
It does. In the microscopic depths,
life bubbles and breeds. At the very
centre of the blackest hole, it shines.
No abyss can stop it. No death can sting.

Grace, eighteen years old

A leap into the world as pool,
a swim around the fringes.

Eyes averted from stern faces,
the boundaries pushing outwards.

Heart consumes what heart desires
and dives towards the bottom.

Closing ears; loath now to hear,
but longing to breathe water.

Yet somehow buoyed up by all
that draws you to the surface.

Lift hands in prayer, avert your eyes;
the boundary pushes outwards.

The current draws you into grace;
these patient arms still hold you.

You are not your own: After Jackie Bartley

I remember how,
months before marriage, I joined a gym,
and after scorching through the summer, training my
body to fit my wedding suit, I would sink
into the cooler waters of the swimming pool,
flailing while others floated, then turning
humbled to the showers where I prepared
my body to be seen, standing
amidst this room of bodies, moon-like,
vast and varied in their imago Dei, where
chests stood tall or caved, hair
grew and receded, and flesh
shrivelled in reminder
to man that he is not God.

                                   Now I seldom
shower without visitors, or calls
on my time for the urgent
needs of childhood; even
the toilet is no refuge. And all
my functions and ablutions,
which were always before You, now take place
before the peering, guileless eyes of my offspring,
and if I ever thought otherwise,
I am not my own,
however I sculpt or hide.

                                    All this
lay before me then, unseen like some
vapour from the Delphic oracle, while on these
public benches beside the showers
a contented senate of seniors table-chattered,
draped in towels like togas, and I

struggled into underwear and jeans as though
unashamed yet always uncertain,
always—even now—counting the cost
of this other-facing life.

Isaiah 11:8 at bath time

Two weeks from being four, my eldest declares
that he doesn't like the "stuff that God does".
What stuff? I ask.
"Like making scary creatures," he says—my son
who delights in killer whales and pretends
to be a blue-ringed octopus, yet knows
the enmity of the snake lurking in grass.

And so bath time leads to Eden: I try
with tired mind and voice shaky from
a day of meltdowns and little sleep
to draw the thread from a garden cursed
to Isaiah, and the child playing by the adder's hole.
"So then," he pauses, sleep nearby,
"I won't be scared of snakes that day?"
No, I say, stroking his face.
The thought is comfort enough today.

Half a story later, eyes close,
while I return to my grown-up fears
and must preach it all again, to me.

Someday All This Will Be Yours

Basalt decks the plain.
You see it dot the earth like a broken wall,
cast up by kilometres of coast crushed when continents split.
Gondwana gone, wastes of Antarctica cleft, sulphur spewed from
seabed;
and so all the grasslands of the West are salted by bluestone,
substance of homes—a hut, roofed with turf; a town to be seen,
when the white men came, then misunderstood, discarded, burnt
—or else a barrier, a wall.

I am the son and heir of all this messy,
teeming stuff: shed, scattered, shattered, spread.
Inheritor of a debt, a crime,
a guilt that what is mine is stolen,
and all this high-heaven-stink that clings to my skin, my genes:
all this
someday will be yours,
my sons who clamour and call in the backseat; all this
tangled stuff of death and dirt, and life,
somehow life,
teeming in it all like a wild
subterranean flow
of grace.

Conversation with my son

At the sink he perches
atop his two-stepped seat to watch
a morning routine that's utter
prose for me, discovery for him:

how I wet
the shaving brush, lather soap,
then smooth the jawline
of my beard, and how
I brush my teeth without
protest, without needing
to eat the toothpaste with each brush.

And then how I open
the mirrored cabinet and take
my pill-cutter, split
Escitalopram in two, and scoop
water into my mouth to swallow.

"What will you swallow, Dad?"
How to answer?
"Medicine," I say, "to help
the chemicals in my brain."

"Maybe," he says, "when I am bigger,
I will take some medicine too."

Oh my heart. "I hope not,"
is all I can say,
"because then you won't have
the sickness I have."

And as talk turns to other
two-year-old things,

my father heart churns
with the weight of this,
while pandemic and cabin fever
test the power of the pills, the rage
of being Dad drives the nerves
that splash water on my morning face.

Hyperecho

*And the peace of God, which passeth all understanding, shall keep
your hearts and minds through Christ Jesus.*

~ Philippians 4:7

Mind often tempest,
I long for the instant of stilling
when Christ shakes off
salty sleep from pin-needled feet and holds
council with the waves and the mast,
commands cumulonimbus to disperse,
wind pressure to cease, and all
this conglomeration of wild to rest
and let waters settle.

Rarely have I seen it.
Well-rehearsed, my mind
can turn the stillest seas to whirlpools,
whipping up a frenzy to rival
a Galilean's worst fear of the abyss.
Waters ripple and I am dropped
through sunlight straight
into childhood's Hadal terrors of night.
The instant's meanest work is to recall
every deepest dread.

Instead, prayer's answer is most often this: not
a thundering voice to quiet every
squall and hurricane, to stem
the rising tsunami; no, but

Christ's reason-defying head
sleeping instead, while
Hell rages all about and the crew
prepare to jettison all but themselves
and Leviathan chuckles at the sport...

Jesus sleeps
and, in a voice like ultrasound,
bids me do the same.
And while I thrash about in oceanic howl,
this is my prayer's best and only answer.
Deep it calls, with its fathom-diving echo.

Bathos

. . .what is the breadth, and length, and depth, and height. . .

~ *Ephesians 3:18*

The apostle Paul, surviving
shipwrecks and knowing the threat
of an unknowable abyss, wrote
of God's love having bathos
the same word Alexander Pope took
to describe a kind of sinking sickness
he despised in inferior verse:

Bathos for depth, as a way of saying,
"How low you've sunk", or denoting
a void of transcendence, an abyss one might
plunge into when trying too hard, or
like a Greek Chorus warning Oedipus
how the ocean depths stand always
as the foil to clutching pride.

My undergraduate ear heard it as a sort of
"bad pathos", or like pathos with a cold. A poet
with congested nose muddling
through clumsy iambs in a tepid bath. But now,
my eldest child obsessed with oceanic zones, I hear
new resonance, imagine instead

the bathypelagic and that
mysterious blue sphere lowered
into unknown midnight depths, finding

creatures more at home in Grimm or Bosch
than our perceptions of science: luminescent
eels like winding electrical cables; fish with circular fangs;
giant fluorescent tubes that prove, somehow, to be worms;
prehistoric coelacanths thought long extinct.

And yet
even this proved to be like wading in the shallows when
that crack in the Pacific floor was found,
tunneling into miles on miles of undiscovered earth,
an upside-down Everest of teeming
dark, unimaginable life,
lurking far, far beneath all reasonable expectation:
simplest of single cells yet infinitely baffling in their
near impossible presence.

When it says
He ascended, must he also have
descended, meaning
plumbed
into unfathomed depths? And was this
descent somehow part of the saving?
And before he rose, did he first plunge an anchor,
binding love with its deathblow to this earth-plunging ooze?

Depths of mercy. Leaden weight of grace.
No hubris sinks this deep; only praise.

Noah's Ark

I.
Delighted by animals, God and rain,
my son finds kinship in Noah's ark,
commentating the story as I leaf through his Bible:
"Rain! Giraffe. Boat. Noah. Wet. Monkeys!"
How to convey what
a rainbow's about, or how I long
for him and his brothers to be
kept safe in the ark
as the flood passes.

II.
After the night's deluge, I spot
a raven atop a traffic light,
tree-branch in beak,
heralding the hope of dry land.
The lights change, I drive ahead.
No flood will overwhelm today.

III.
This afternoon he found
some joyfully fluffy infant ducks
in a book and, excited, pointed them out:
"Clucklings!" he exclaimed, and how I wished
that our language could change
to make them be clucklings forever.

IV.
Reading a story of sloths, I asked,
"Do you think there were sloths in Noah's ark?"
While he gave this all his toddler's thought,

I amused myself with images of
the haste with which Noah packed the ark
the sloths sabotaging all his speed,
yet saved, thank God, all the same.

III
Breath

And so the father turns at evening to collating an abstraction of sounds, like a collage of morphemes, a catalogue of phonemes, the signs of first speech, earliest language, or the remnants of one reduced to only grunts and plosives

and sounds are at once marvellous and concrete, meaningless and definite, like the wonder of his children's names, like the first sound of a baby's cry, or the agony of love

and yet the sounds when assembled lose meaning, only the utterance carrying something purposeful, as though they were feathers that did not belong in his box but to air or the spots on a butterfly's wing,

only in flight, only when released as prayer do they catch the spirit's breath and turn into life—

Listening for air

Before sleep, I creep down
the hall, pry open the children's door
and stand between the cots and wait
to hear three channels of breath flowing through.
And sometimes, the twins' so often in sync,
the three distinct strands hard to catch,
I move in and place a listening hand
to catch chest's silent rise and fall
and in the stillness feel the air
gather roaming breath around me
as threads to weave into a prayer.

Pharmacology

Persistent low mood. Chronic insomnia.
Generalised anxiety. Panic attacks.
Prescribe Avanza (generic: Mirtazapine).
Side effects may include
vertigo, dryness in mouth,
decreased/increased libido (take your pick).
Some sounds may be unusually loud.
Be warned also that crossing timezones
may screw up all progress made
and though at first it heals your sleep
in increased doses this could change.
Don't say that you weren't warned.
(I was not warned.)

Invasive thoughts. Compulsive hands.
Mild trichotillomania.
The voice of the devil in your pounding heart.
Prescribe Zoloft. No better?
Try Escitalopram instead.
The slow adjust; withdrawal wanes.
We hope it's therapeutic soon.
Dosage creeps up to the max;
normal's more or less okay
(aside from how it's always not,
and yearly blood tests, ECGs,
mild threats in cholesterol,
not to mention the taptaptapping
that always lurks inside your limbs.
But since you sleep and do not feel
every day so much like hell,
you take the best that you can get.)
Is this the best that you can get?

And now we meet Venlafaxine.
Is the dosage right? Not quite?
Have the years of Lexapro
destroyed your heart?
Will this too outstay its use?
And have the years of therapy done their job?
Not yet. Not yet.
Time to scrape your soul again.

You will not fear the terrors of the night

Behold, I stand at the door, and knock . . .

~ *Revelation 3:20*

I.
Behold. The old house
by the bay creaks and thumps in the darkness.
Though my grandparents reassure me
(*Old houses are noisy; nothing to fear*)
the possums hiss like murderers
and the walls groan like the slain.

And the door—behold.
Do you hear the tapping?
It persists. I ignore, yet who else
would stand at the bedroom door to knock?
Draped in night, I lie paralysed,
fearful of rising yet agonising that I
have left my saviour at the door and, bad host
that I am, have failed to let him in.

Darkness drags. Devil digs in claws. Endless
night comes to eventual end.
Adult self cannot recall how it all resolves.
Jacob rises with hip out of socket.
Grandparents greet at breakfast and all
seems well again, though somehow askew.

Jesus is silent, unknocking,

yet lives with me nonetheless.
Behold. *Be held*, the spirit whispers.
You walk in faith another day, but this—
the pestilence in the darkness, stalking—
takes decades to unlearn.

II.
Like the way your brain recalls
the schoolyard chant—*Bloody Mary! Bloody Mary!*—
while you wash your hands at night before
the mirror. Unsummoned, the words persist,
become an onslaught. Must you
say them aloud to give them power? Or is
the unbidden, sieging thought enough
to summon a vengeful queen from her sleep?

Horrified at the brain's demonic frenzy, you run,
bed only small comfort when the dread dwells in you.
You will not fear the terrors of the night, you are told.
Yet pestilence is hard to thwart
when it stalks inside your mind
and has no substance at all.

III.
Insubstantial, it nevertheless
clutches at you some nights with all
the talons of Hell. Whether

you call for help and try
to give account to the haggard parent,
the baffled brother, for these nighttime cries;

or, as years pass and you must
"put away childish things", you learn
to be discrete, staying silent in your terror,

it comes to feel familiar, as though
when darkness descends, takes shape and walks in,
you are greeting a friend, and this

too has power to terrify, for what
kind of child is a friend of the dark?
And who else knows the devil's face,

even in such dim light?

A Work of Love

I remember,
late twenties, Kierkegaard's
Works of Love
on my lap before bed
and the blazing words *You shall love*
making brain quake at the thought,
the risk that loving entailed.
Brain forms its pathways to protect,
weaves blankets to hide its tenderest dark.
Love would see brain's secret places opened,
would shine its torch on the hidden self,
the parts I had cloaked for fear of them.
Brain shook, and writhed,
in the fury of being known.
The shaking would rage
before passing.

Now, six years married,
children sleeping down the hall,
I find again
my secret places shaken,
my tightly woven
comfort stretched beyond
recognition
by You, the stormy and tender
God of Isaiah, finding
feet once more at abyss' edge
knowing only
one way to leap, and certain
that brain's fabric must be stretched
before it can heal, knowing

Yours are the depths
and the depths of me are wide open,
naked, before Your knowing eye.
Knowing I
must plunge in You,
I quiver. Brain quakes
before it can be held. O shake me.
Hold me until I am whole.

For my son

All my dirt rises to the surface.
This takes a servanthood that I do not hold
and so I grasp
at old roots of self deep-buried in peatbogs
of years gone by
as, some vestige of me, I walk through the night,
useless yet needed, no moment to hide.

Gathered in sleep, or lack of it, you know
none of this.
One day, one day—
you too will feel the pull
that one way says "Love" and the other "Me".
Now you simply fight between
the need for sleep and the need to gasp
all the world into eyes learning to see.
I yearn to see.
Have patience, my child.
I am blinded by me.

Little Brother

Will this be your first? they ask.
So what do we say?
That before you was another
who got lost on the way?
Unviable, out of place,
yet loved, oh how loved.
How do we name the agony
of hidden loss, and a treasure
held only by us?

No: not only us. For
before there was you,
or me, or your mother,
there was Life.
And what Life: older than stars,
yet one of us,
made flesh among us.

What a journey this Life made,
across multiverse to wait
nine months like you do now
to come out to this atmosphere,
to beat and to breathe.

What truths this Life knew,
our little lost one now knows too:
Eternity's arms, the comfort of perfect
face-to-face knowing,
the absence of tears.

What tears we have shed.

We will tell you, one day;
one day hold you, and show you
how Love can remain.

First Spark

Dinosaur cranes wander the Docklands plain:
in metal skin, they stand still and wait—
for prey? Or do dinosaurs appreciate
the quiet of the newfound day? Contained
in corrugated homes, our food, our wealth
line the docks (some man's work, another's play);
such a thing is life, in sparkle and fade
of dawn and old age, in sickness and health.
Fate will take each species, Auden said, yet life
is here to show you if you live. First light,
weakest spark; the day is new and might succumb.
Blink and miss an age going out of sight.
These two pink lines declare that life has come;
I clutch them in my fist now as I drive.

For a neverborn

We never brought you home. The day we met,
you began to leave us. No joy when we saw
your minute form, white upon black screen—more
grief than gladness, amidst decisions, wet
with all the weight of this. How out of place
you were, our child. But oh, how much we'd longed –
how vast your loss—how voidlike—how prolonged. . .
How partially we now see. Soon, with face-
to-face recognition, we will know you—
we who, though stunted, have loved and grown you.
Baptised with tears, embraced by our heartbeats,
you shall never know incompleteness.
When you awake at the steps of His feet,
you will know life by seeing His likeness.

Homecoming

We lit you a candle, Advent-purple,
and sang in our darkest hour of wait.
We sowed seeds in messages of shared grief
and watched as some returned fruitful, some void.
Even with all of our best efforts employed,
we screamed at the ceiling in mad disbelief
and doubted to see that flame kindled. Great
is His faithfulness, great the gap from steeple
to heart; not even Job's counselors spoke
some silent times. Yet home begins in this:
opening a room to the messiness
of footprints and of dirty fingers' poke-
poke where our frailties are. And family starts
when it puts its soiled feet up in our hearts.

A Mindlessness Prayer

These days when all of the socks are odd
and all your thoughts are scrambled eggs
and, try as you might to talk to God,
nothing much makes any sense,

for the rubbish awaits in noisome piles,
the bills are due and so's the tax
and the laundry measures its depth in miles
and the devil has pains for idle backs—

unjumble yourself in a heap at Christ's feet;
ramble and rant to the maker of ants
and all that creeps the planet, replete
with all its tangled, unnecessary plants;

rejoice to be useless and childlike and weak;
rejoice that you cannot make anything work;
rejoice and delight that the end of the week
will come round regardless of what you deserve;

delight to know this: though mindless you are,
He who is mindful of you holds the stars.

Presence

My youngest, caught
    somewhere between waking and sleep,
clutches my fingers one by one like
    each is a rope pulling him back
to safety, or rest—or like
    a blind man reading meaning
and personhood in
    the grooves and bumps in a hand
        a face,
holding onto the comfort
    in the grasping dark,
of my unseen
presence

My Monastery

I.

My son breathes morning
on my sleeping face.
The day still amniotic, I
drift into fog
and slow-unfolding light.

Clutched by a sweaty palm
I lift
pieces of myself and place
my snotty fist into
Your hair and breathe.

II.

Order unravels quickly
from sleepy first breath to
outbreak of chaos.
I cannot control
the unfolding of the day, but God
of the singularity and
multiplicity: teach me
single-heartedness. May I
take this moment
to listen.

III.

Outside myself I see
my own unravelling, my own
dirt seep into the cracks
of my family.

Within myself I feel
the pull, the call
to rise from the dirt
and breathe You.

Day tests what morning resolved;
in resolution's coming and going, make
these words more than words. Take
my liberty, my entire will.

I know You will.

IV.

The day had gone on long enough.
First the Pharisees and their questions,
then the intruding children,
then the camel and the needle's eye,

so that, when they cried out,
"Who then can be saved?" it was
as much from the weariness of the day's
debates as the thought that riches
could keep an earnest man from heaven.

And so, right when
all their careworn sandals seemed
not worth the effort, He looked
into eyes and said, "What's impossible
for man is possible for God."
What then? Could God lift
the labour-sick soul and write
new possibility in its genes?

In the midst of the burden
and the striving, this truth:

Be small. Be like a child.
Be less so I may be more.

V.
And in the noise of the day
the clutter of corridors
the chaos bouncing on schoolroom floors

in the percussion of the evermoving task

your soul waits in silence,
in silence asks
for the silent attention to find
the focused moment in the flurried,

the whole in the fragment,
the nomad mind alert
to the opportune present,
breaking open.

V.

Everything breaks,
is broken, or
sticks like porridge underfoot.
Voice grows tired;
heart turns wild
at the endless, savage
price of love.
Crushed underfoot,
I learn Eden and Golgotha
while I wipe the floor again.
Body breaks, is broken,
tomorrow is new.

VI.

In all this, glory.
It breathes in your face and messes
your hair and says,
"You." It looks
in your eyes and twists
your insides out to be
brushed and scrubbed by bedtime,
sore
and loveworn,
glorious.

VII.

At the going-down and the slowing
taper me Lord but lose me not
to the fading of the light.
Within silence let me
O God entrust all
my daytime sight
to render You
Lord more
bright.

Grace, twenty-eight years old

Weighed down with all
the sheep's clothing I
have daily donned,
this wolf-face I
deny but own,
and all my other faces too;

smothered in
self and this
stink-to-heaven stench of all
that I have scattered, sown, now reap,
decked in dead flowers,
sprouting pride,

staring in the face of true
holiness—a lion on
the prowl; a white
and fiery Day,
consuming my
protective night:

and then: a hand
to guide into
a fire which does not destroy;
the gentle rising of the sun;
the lion's mane lowered to me;
the shepherd dying for the wolf.

IV
Life

Bodies like words carry history.
Archaeological in their layers,
you can trace in them our eras and aeons,
can measure our years
in the rings around our trunks,

                can track
the meteoric collision that sent
particles of us flying into
the sky for years enough to block
the sun,

                can spot
the new life that burst,
first as amoeba, then
as dazzling spectacles of life,
from the protozoic soil
      of this newly graced beginning.

Who are you? you ask
to this emerging, teeming life.
I am you, it replies, as it stretches its limbs,
only older and younger
than you could ever have dreamed.

Riddle I

When it opens
like a chasm—the question
asked in your stomach's
pit—you find

seldom an answer, only
a longing for one, or
an apology for
its absence

like I did the day I,
ten years old, saw
a man glare at me as
we drove nonchalant past him.

He stood
at the caravan park
barbecues and mouthed,
Him! at my face, or so

I fancied, and when
I told my brother he called
me paranoid, and yet
there was truth

nonetheless
in the way the words
clamored
foghornlike

a warning
in the air,
the question implied,
as though

I must justify
my presence here,
and I
have never

trod the earth
easily since.

Dianoia

That the eyes of your understanding may be lightened, that ye may
know what the hope is of his calling, and what the riches of his
glorious inheritance is in the Saints. . .

~ *Ephesians 1:18, Geneva Bible*

Before dinner my children play
"Pretend Church", a wild
and varied game consisting
of dress-ups, piano presets and snatches
of half-remembered liturgy,
improvised worship songs with
key phrases scattered like
a jazz singer's scats: *mighty!*
Saviour! Lord Jesus Christ!
Faith at first is part
instinct, part performance,
an improvised trying-on-for-size, or
a toddler testing out a new dress-up kit.
But then—as mind enlarges to make
space for growing truth,
no longer an act; the words become
not performative, more like breath,

like the way,
as a college student, I devoured Ephesians,
absorbing Pauline clauses highlighter in hand
inhaling every verb and adverb as though
mind atrophied without it. *This is you,*
it said. *Now live.* Decades gone,
faith sometimes worn rice-paper-thin,

while my children dance I take
my old study Bible from the shelf and leaf
its weathered, underlined pages. *Welcome
to church!* my youngest shouts. Welcome.
May the eyes of my heart be enlightened;
may You highlight new life again.

After Losing

And what if, in the end, you lost it all?
In the poorly timed decision,
the negligent hurry,
in missing the moment for the undoing click?
What if, in a swift dazzle of technology, all
your acts and monuments fell down a drain
never to be found or known again?

Would you, then, wake up at sunrise
to find that, in spite of it all, the wattle-birds still
have their insistent call, and there still
are the honeyeaters in the bottlebrush hedge?
Would you find a familiar coffee pot on the stove,
pattering feet wandering the hallway in their sleeping bag,
and thoughts—new day thoughts—to replace the old?

Perhaps, in a moment of quiet, you might find yourself
turning to the persistence of ink on paper and scrape
some hesitant symbols, soon words, soon poems,
and see new combinations, hear new
assemblages sound, and find
in the rhythms of your pen, in
the undulations of thought, something which
perhaps could owe its very iambs,
its steady pulsations across page
to the loss that yesterday crippled you.

Holy Mess

Sanctify the compost heap
where I trudge in dark with the day's dank scraps.
Sanctify the living stench,
soil's second chance,
barren fig-tree's friend.

Sanctify the dishes piled
on piles around the cluttered sink.
Sanctify the time it takes
to scrub and dry,
to sort and stack.

Sanctify numb fingers, ice
on windscreen that delays the day,
brittle tests when patience is small.
Sanctify mess,
sanctify time.

Sanctify unholy pain;
sanctify this senselessness
that drives me to the end of me
and sends me to Your feet.

Aves Australiae

All the birds of the freeway

I journey between factories and billboards and trees;
needles of light pierce the morning sky,
and in the east the vermilion city wakes.

Spanning the distance, birds fly in sequence,
sweeping sheets, kites, giant gulls across the horizon.
When I arrive I will be static, and spark at friction
from those who start their day unawares.

If I cannot have flight, O God, let me kneel;
we deny You with every passive grumble,
each scant refusal of Your song.

Afternoon Flight

A willy wagtail, was it?
Perhaps, but no time to check *What Bird Is That?*
as it wags its way through lanes at lights,
a truck here turning, there a foot
compressing asphalt.
                              Yes,
I have seen its tail—proud tuft of feathers –
pluckily braving the afternoon rush,
and seen it hover, tentative,
just above Old Geelong Road,
as though not quite prepared to fly.
Sometimes it slips
beneath my sight, and then

it darts, as though to dare the traffic.
None destroy it, yet most—unaware –
continue changing lanes as they
would on any normal Friday.
Stationary, I see its tail
greet the traffic, weekend-bound;
such smallness seems almost defiant here.
Is grace defenceless as we drive?
No: cars resume, as green returns,
yet willy wags the tail, and faith
skips the traffic's plight.

Music for Children's Choir

Headphone-bound, children sing as I round the corner.
The nonchalance of late morning traffic greets
a flutter of flight—black and white feathers—
painting the street in uncontrolled strokes:
a rise, a swoop, a leap, a fall.

Ballet-graced, yet deadly in its implications:
too wild, too close to the turmoil of wheels.
Cars persevere. Children sing:
Veni Domine, et noli tardare.
O come; no delay. Around the tyre-tracks of the day,
a magpie fights death as it flies.

Crow

Content to miscomprehend, my flock flew
across the seas and stole
like cuckoos another's nest.

Feathering with the fetters of home, they named
all they saw as though they never left: magpie, raven, magpie-lark.

Some sparrows and wrens, though distinct,

had at least the likeness of an English wood.
Presumption plumps and plumes. I must train
my eyes to see subtlety, to greet

humbly what great-great-grandfather scorned,
to thank the old crow who cleans the carrion,
ancient in beauty, no two feathers the same.

Passerine

An English friend describes
Australian signage as saying,
more or less, *You might die!*

And true, the messaging is clear,
even down to the floodwater warning as I take
a quiet amble by the river, startled

by the silhouette of a body drowning
on an innocent yellow marker by the path.
Memento Mori. Any time, anywhere.
                                    But is it

the constancy of the threat, or our
characteristic nonchalance, our bravado
that demands we have all these reminders?

First settlers carved their name in the soil with claims
that they had won against the hostile south. And on
the myth-making goes. Yet blue wrens dance over

kangaroo grass, and somewhere a plucky
orange-bellied parrot turns north across the strait,
defiant to the last. I pause,

scanning gums' tops where a kite dangles,
orange, yellow and white like a feather
dropped by some exotic creature hovering

between here and heaven. Hell is
what we've made in the souls of others:
children fighting, drinkers on the park bench.

Passing, I take stock of my damage.
Soon I will drive away. Now
I pray to give grace where I gather.

Feathers unlike and alike all flutter
as Heaven heaves this living
flock together.

Northbound on Derrimut

The old chief Derrimut died at the Melbourne Benevolent Asylum,
on Wednesday last. Derrimut was the last chief of those tribes of
aborigines who were encamped in the neighborhood of the Yarra
when Mr Fawkner and the first settlers arrived here. It will be
remembered that Derrimut saved the first settlers from being
massacred by the blacks, as he gave them timely warning of the
intended attack.

~ *The Age, Fri 29th April 1864*

Named as it is after him,
I drive this road picturing him,
along with Benbow and Billibellary,
walking past warehouses and
housing estates to find
Fawkner and associates
to warn of impending attack.

But it did not happen here and only
the name is preserved, to say
Once he would have walked here,
while the walls that the settlers built—
dry stone, now considered
of *historical and aesthetic significance, and*
in some cases, of social and archaeological
or scientific significance—remain as monuments,
stone by stone, where they first stood.

And so
life grows, as the billboard has it,

in and around the walls we built,
the continuous present turned
to memorial, the past remembered
as immoveable stone.
Thistles grow
where land lies fallow, waiting
for steamroller or plough,
or the town planner's dividing knife.
Traffic chokes the morning air,
and Derrimut, name robbed
of life and motive, calls out:
I protected you—
for what?

I carry my own geography's shame:
the main street of Colac named for the forebear
who showed *the blackfellow, at first hostile*
the power of a white man's weapons, and
the strength of a white man's heart,
firing, the Colac Herald proudly reports,
his white man weapons *into*
the yelping curs who had
destroyed the ewes of pure blood and high price,
brought with such trouble to Colac's shores.

Dingos do not howl here, but
the shores are troubled still
by the price of blood, the price
of destruction. The day's
surface lies more settled
than the past can accept.

Indicators blink.
Day turns its own way
into forgetting.

Settling

No spear wound or anything of the sort to recount to you, but
live a quiet, peaceable, sober, monotonous, pleasant life, without
bothering anybody or anybody bothering me.

~ Hugh Murray, in a letter to his sister, 17th May, 1837

At first—having chosen
lands remarkably like home, with their
verdant hills and autumn rains,
the country *ideal for a sheep run,*
beautiful
scenery, soft gliding streams and oh!
you never saw such grass,

and ducks! unexpectedly ducks
to roast for tea—it all seems
surprisingly ordinary, as though
you hadn't leapt
the antipodes to find yourself grazing here.
Of course there's the fact
of the miscoloured swans—who would
believe that swans could be black?—
and the sojourn in heavenly Hobart where
your father found a climate ripe for grapes, began
pressing and selling the fruit of this foreign
yet familiar soil.

And there's the dry.
When you encounter the dry, you know
you're far from Edinburgh; and that heat

68

that scalds like home never did. And when
you care to admit, there's also
the natives, with their
dingoes threatening your flocks, and

the other things besides, which you cannot
possibly tell your sister. Better to simply
relate the misfortunes
that beset your dinnertime, how
hard it is to *boil a piece of beef, stew a duck, and
make tea in all the same pot*, not to mention when
there's *no ducks to stew*. Add, for honesty's sake,
a harmless *etc.*, for that can cover
a multitude of foreign things, the ways
this strange land yields things stranger yet
inside you.

You've eaten their
fish, found in the traps what your settler
brain can scarcely compute. You've seen
skin smeared with fat, and thought
it must mean something devilish. You've killed
dogs to atone for the death of sheep.
You've written letters calling for
action, but never, you swear, fired a single
angrily aimed shot. Not yourself.
Nor seen one fired. Thank God,
not that.

Nor with
the years can you explain
how hundreds of strange bodies have
dwindled over the years to a handful. Perhaps
you say, over your widening pot, your
ever-growing stove, perhaps
the land merely favoured your sheep.

Some details
of your prosperity cannot
be explained; you marvel
that it should be so. Yet here it is:
all this bounty blessing
your hearth. Do you recall
the nights when there were
no ducks? Few they were. You had
them *at least four times a week.*

                                     Yet that,
when you think back, was the worst
you could say of those early brazen days,
that sometimes—rarely—
you had no duck for tea.

Life Beneath

Berrin (Mt Gambier), Boandik Country

Under the city, a tour guide who,
if not secluded away in regional Australia, should
have starred in Werner Herzog films, recounts

the myriad ways that this
porous calcified roof above us could,
for all we know, tumble down on our heads,

being, as he delights to tell us,
essentially "nothing", just air, like clouds,
like ourselves.

Underground rivers, flowing from raindrops,
filtered through limestone over aeons, finally
gushing out of this chalky coast

to the Southern Ocean as though
longing for the frozen continent rent
from its side. We too are porous.

So is our past to
the Boandik, recalling
Ancient cataclysm, as though it happens

every day, and it does. Ground that was
certain for millennia, carved
into parcels for this governor and that.

Rifts open. Land is pulled away from home.
Home moves.
"Over there," he points.

"See those two set-squares?"
Perpendicular like
a cross, they mark

where the rock now stands, the slightest
change in which could make
the city above us plunge.

"If the cross stands," he declares, "we're alright."
And the Creator, father of flesh and volcanoes, nods, says,
Yes. But not as you imagine.

This shall be mine

Next come the York Plains, which surpassed in beauty anything I have yet seen, but when the Salt Pan Plains opened to my view I was struck with astonishment. Here thousands of acres are crying, "Come and possess me"...

~ *From the diary of John Maule Hudspeth, 12th October, 1822*

Being "anxious, like most young men, to see
something of the world before settling down",
John Maule Hudspeth, doctor by trade yet without
the thirty guineas to secure his diploma, set off
first north, aboard a whaling ship, from which
the lay preacher judged
the pagan lives his northern neighbours led, bled
hypochondriacs, spotted unicorns and preached
Christ to the "poor benighted souls" aboard
the ship. When disappointed by fellow
Christians, he declared "human nature" still
the same "human nature in the most
remote corner of the world". He spied
"Esquimaux Indians", declared them dependent
on the same whales his vessel sought, and thought
nothing of their nature or souls.

                              And when,
older, married, disappointed by England, he set off
this time Southward, he found
acres of fertile lands begging
to be possessed, and asked
no questions of the "native" who "suddenly

appeared out of the bush and threw
a spear" at his "favourite dog, while in
the act of killing a kangaroo". Withstanding
shipwreck, bushrangers, wild
tigers and devils attacking his flock, he built
his home by the new Jordan, the walls of this
southern Jericho invisible to his English eye.
His family spread its roots far and wide,
his labours rewarded, obstacles tumbled...

Years later, having seen
the world, his lands now prospering,
home and hearth expanding,
his diary closed in silence, only
a letter remaining to thank
George Augustus Robinson, Chief
Protector of the Aborigines, for "relieving
the community of Van Diemen's Land from
the attacks of the Aborigines; and for
the talent exhibited by him in conciliating
the Savage Tribes, and effecting
without bloodshed their removal from
this Colony to Flinders Island."
History knows how Robinson protected;
Flinders Island is a bloody footnote.
And John Maule Hudspeth, body and mind worn
by the strain of the Arctic and his
pioneering days, finally settled, "incurable"
in his "mental decay", in New Norfolk,
a town first built for felons, now
a resting place for the bruised of mind.

His wife, her story never told, died
with Jesus' name on her lips.

Other Bodies

First he thought, *Bone of my bone, flesh of my flesh,*
and the dance of likeness and difference thrilled through his flesh,
this body so like his own yet cleft
where his joined and stretched, curved
and peaked where his was smooth

and they yearned from the first to recover their distance,
to live in constant merging and departing
and their morningfresh flesh knew no shame
in its pure exposure.

But after fruit turned bitter and sour on the tongue,
and fig-leaves then beasts' skins failed to hide shame,
they turned first to shelter in dark corners,
always retreating, always pursuing the other, until
tired nights with their last goat-skins soiled as diapers, they took

refuge in recrimination: "He's self-righteous like you."
"Well, look at his face. He has your birthmark.
Mark my words: he'll have your temper, too, your way
of claiming you've only got crumbs left to give."

And on, on, into exiled night they raged,
until the clefts and grooves, curves and tufts
that once delighted now seemed
one with all they despised,
a mirror of their own naked disgrace.

Yet still in their hatred they ached
to throw off disguise and be bare,
be co-ribbed again as though
stolen fruit had never soured difference.

Adam Exposed: After Julia Kasdorf

When Adam, no fellow found fit to complete him,
Fell asleep, alone, God chose
To diminish him before finishing what he lacked,
Taking from him before making for him,
That he might always wear his need humbly:
A missing rib; a tail between his legs,
Purposeless unless connected and giving.
And God chose to slow him, to teach him slowness,
That he might serve not rule;
That he might learn to hold
Power and powerlessness alike
In ever-giving love.

Such was the plan. May our bodies relearn it.
After all Eden's evergreens have autumned from memory,
And all we have is this mess of ourselves,
After Cain enabled all brothers to murder,
After David's eyes took what was not his,
After Noah Lot Judah all made nakedness shame:
May we remember the hand that takes to complete,
That breaks and scars to heal.

And woe to the Adam who, rueing his weakness,
Figleafs his dangling shame with control.
And woe to the Adam who, hating his lack,
Curses the body that cleaves to make whole.

We are such stuff

At first a word denied me, being,
like "nice" or "good", the refuge
of the linguistically lazy,
Shakespeare alone allowed

its use, when that colonising
magician Prospero fancies
himself and his henchmen
the stuff of dreams.

Until
in a Chemistry class
in Switzerland, I am
arrested by the simplicity of words

for familiar substances, rendered
new by their naked naming:
Wasserstof - the stuff of water.
Kohlstof - the stuff of coal.

How rich the world then seemed,
every ordinary thing now teeming
with its own vast array of
electrons orbiting atoms,

the simplest forms combining,
rearranging, like
children gleefully rising
on shoulders and legs to form

an interwoven pyramid,

a lattice, simplicity making
abundant complexity;
the stuff of life. The stuff of us.

Body In Flight

Wounded, the body runs all the same.
Ligaments reject tendons;
balls deny sockets' value.
Cornea declares war on Retina
and the ear beats its own drum.
Because I am not a hand—yells the elbow,
and the spleen,
silent, forgotten, ponders
its purpose. *You think you've
got it bad,* mouths Appendix,
while Biceps and Triceps achieve
accidental unity,
forcing body into motion,
into flight.

Hovering between
dream and action, bones
grind against each other,
moaning
in an agony of reluctant teamwork,
learning, all the same,
each other's grains and curvatures,

and somehow—this, at least, remains,
will remain.

Astronomy

You might think it would humble us to know
   at the end of all our knowing that, for all
this knowing, we are immeasurably   small.
You might think   the sheer expanse, the sheer scale
  of all that we name   Universe   might blow
  our very sense of union.   That we call
"known"   what keeps evading scientific thrall
  (after all our knowing) only goes to show
that, while we think we can admire stars,
  they do not give a damn.   We are in truth
mere dots within their cosmic braille.
                What are we
that we are mindful of ourselves? By far
  better than knowing is to be known,   mere youths
   beneath an ancient love   we cannot see.

Neurochemical Prayer

If after years you leave my body and I
must make a home for another way of thinking,
go easy on these axons and dendrites;
make smooth the pathways between
trigger and thought. May the links
these trees and branches forge
in the soil of my soul be always kind,
and may I wake to find
my brain no longer warring with
the grooves I find inside my life;
and may
I no longer wish scars in being on my face.
May I wake to find my every hole now Whole.
May the dreaming of my living
be a carving of a life that freely breathes.

The Jolt, the Life: A fractured sonnet

Having been looked at by God, I had to and have to look at God.

~ Søren Kierkegaard, Journal

You: how can I call you by familiar names?
Only Thou seems fitting;   yet You invade
     space,   time,   as though   next to me,   as though
                                                          plain.
Yet You are not plain: You assault,   You raid
though never seen;   You never seem   so clear
as when unclear,

                              as when,
                         unlimited,
You stride above   the limits of our spheres.
With one look   from You,   our world's
                                                          up
                                                     ended;

Living *coram Deo* is   to live
                       within,   without,   the leap
                       of faith   of doubt
jolting sense   to   senselessness.
                                                     Revive,
     O One who gives   who takes;   turn out
     our involuted selves   and show us how
     to live   before You,

          in eternal   now.

82

Resurrection Bread

I.

What neglect killed, we try to build again
Taking such simple things as flour, water,
Empty jar on a windowsill,
And in emptiness awaiting the miracle,
Futile as it seems.

II.

Leaves tinge yellow as I stir
This fundamental stuff to mix with air.
Daily this act of faith, this trust, while
The one who calls Himself bread
Stirs my substance too.

III.

Do you understand this new leaven growing here?
It is not like the old one that puffs at the first
Compliment but shrivels in the cool of night:
No, this one's wild, daily renewing, bidding you discard
All that does not bring life.

IV.

By Thursday have you begun to doubt?
Has this whole rising enterprise begun to seem
Implausible? Have past failures and the exhaustion
Of daily removing deadweight begun to feel futile?
Friday looms. Sunday waits.

V.

Does today feel furthest from the miracle?
You can remember the jubilation bubbling like Hosanna,

Now only gasps of air. Do not watch.
Better to turn away, forget how He held up bread
And said, "Remember me."

VI.
In the pause between defeat and victory
There is a cusp of quiet where
We may recall the words of promise, may despair,
May watch closely for signs of life,
May forget to breathe.   Breathe.

VII.
Sealed at first like a tomb—not with death
But its own bubbling life—it must be prised
Open to reveal this burst of vitality.
In such ordinary stuff You whisper, "Yes.
And bodies too."

Prime

Being, as my students kindly advise me, past mine,
I grow accustomed now to seeing:

Stomach slouching when back is straight.
Grey snowtipping the hairs of my beard.
Smile lines, worry lines, whatever lines creasing eyes.
And the way my hair lands like a combover on a windy day.

These I also find:
Heart slouching at lost opportunity.
Fists clenching at time wasted.
Patience waning with constant complaining.
And the sinking sense that dreams
however starward their gaze
may not be what the cricket promised.

And these too:
Some noises growing dimmer that I might
better hear the voice that says
Get over yourself, Pullar.
Spirit growing as flesh slackens.
The speck in my eye looming
larger than your log.
The expanding lines of grace.

Breathbodyprayer

*. . .that form of prayer in which the soul makes use of the members
of the body to raise itself more devoutly to God. In this way the
soul, in moving the body, is moved by it.*

~ *The Nine Ways of Prayer of Saint Dominic*

Fooled by the body's misfirings—
the thought misdirected; the brain
connecting anguish to the neutral moment—
you cannot pray, for every
earnest ascent is duped by the pounding
head that cries out, *Terror, terror
on every side.* And you,
longing for peace where there
is no peace, cannot spy the waiting,
pumping heart that welcomes,
that is already here, is open.

So prayer, at these times, is as much
a breath as a hand outstretched,
an air-parched mouth gulping as it clutches clouds.
And while the body,
in its movement, stretches
its wild, warring muscles,
it wrestles and settles

encased behind the billowing
ribs of its maker,
who did not despise these scars.

Arms II

When every force of hell drags with its hooks
And all the voices lie and shout and scream
That all is lost and all has died;

When knees buckle under the strain
And the motion of praying is not prayer at all,
Only the dull screams of something on fire;

When the words that we mouth are barely words
And the hope that we clutch at is scarcely hope
But the frail refuge of the truly lost:

Hold me. Your arms are too vast for me to see,
Too gentle for me to feel; hold me,
In your imperceptible arms, firm through all my wildest fears.

And when the earth has died and gone,
May I then be found somehow,
Impossibly safe in all that You Are.

Hold me. Carry me. Hold me.

Grace, thirty-eight years old

Yet still
You are with me, like
the children who return
again again
however I—
sleep-deprived and proud—
may have spurned them

and like
the floorboards
that remain despite
our stomping, despite
all our spinning like earths in this
chaotic family orbit
You

remain
and hold me
silent
electromagnet, hold
in Your constancy, in
the firmness of
Your ground.

How to be a good man

First, befriend
the dizzying disquiet that attends
not knowing everything.
It will unsettle
as though you have lost half a limb or misplaced
that tiny vestibular bone in your ear.
Be unsettled. And second,
when unsettled,
settle with yourself to fix nothing.
Do nothing.
Not lazily, like a sloth before the tv,
but with the determined silence of a hermit.
Third, do not be a hermit. No-one needs
your pious absence. Or, if you must,
be the hermit pulled against his wishes
into the cathedral. Refuse the bishop's seat.
Instead, sit—fourthly—on the floor and ask,
"What do you need me to know?" Then let
the wave of your unknowing wash away pride.
Repent. Repeat. Repent.

Riddle II

For when it opens
like a chasm
You are
in the chasm.

When it whispers
in silence
You are
in the silence.

When knowing
splits,
You know
all this.

When the question
shatters,
You are
the reply.

*

And when I find
myself at
the end
of myself, I find

myself end
and at these frayed
ends hangs not
my end

but where
opening up into
failure I open in
You –

Compline

Now and in the diminishing of the light

I have left much unraveled,
left many frayed ends ragged.

And in the moment before
mind disengages from the day and idles
in the space between days

I see
the faces of all I have failed
the hands of all I have not loved as myself—
have not loved myself.

As day tapers into waxen rest—
now and at the going down of the sun

I have left much undone
I have left much undone

and I will rise
threefold-God my refuge
to the battle raging still,
the battle won.

Gratis

Caught out again,
the senselessness surprising always:
that way your arms have now of reaching
and how your smile beckons;

And me with my hands still dirty,
clothes dishevelled, face not there,
turning now aside from you
towards the corner, somehow proud.

Senseless and surprising with your
periscopic, plumbing gaze
and eyes that touch in silent hoping,
fingers like your perfect scars;

the offer of your warmest shoulders
and these reserves of purest grace:
deep and deep the wounds that feed it,
free and flowing beyond belief.

Notes

"Vespers: After Louise Glück" was inspired by the sequence of poems entitled "Vespers" from Louise Glück, The Wild Iris. New York: Ecco, 1993.

"You Are Not Your Own: After Jackie Bartley" was inspired by the poem "Baptism" from Jackie Bartley, Ordinary Time. New York: Spire, 2007.

"Bathos" takes its name from the Greek word for depth used by Alexander Pope in his essay Peri Bathous, Or the Art of Sinking in Poetry (1728) satirizing the poetry of his day.

"Northbound on Derrimut": the quotes about dry stone walls come from the Planning and Environment Act 1987 Panel Report Wyndham Planning Scheme Amendment C209 Dry Stone Walls, 13 January 2016. Quotes about Hugh Murray come from the obituary for his wife, Elizabeth Murray, The Colac Herald, Tuesday 14 June 1893, p.3.

"Adam Exposed: After Julia Kasdorf" was inspired by the poem "Eve's Striptease" from Julia Kasdorf, Eve's Striptease. Pittsburgh: University of Pittsburgh Press, 1998.

www.ingramcontent.com/pod-product-compliance
Lightning Source LLC
Chambersburg PA
CBHW070017110426
42741CB00034B/2080